WICCA

ESSENTIAL PRACTITIONER'S GUIDE
TO WICCA FOR BEGINNER'S, WICCAN
SPELLS & WITCHCRAFT

Jessica Jacobs

Wicca

Wicca

Table of Contents

Introduction - What Is Wicca

Despite what you may initially think, Wicca is an extremely calm, harmonious and well-balanced lifestyle which encourages living in harmony with the divine and everything that exists.

Wicca is a faith system which promotes living in harmony with the world and appreciating it for what it is; taking in the sunrise or appreciating the beauty and inspiration from the setting sun, or from how the light plays in the forest, the moon as it shines in the night sky, or how the meadow looks as though it is ablaze when the first rays of the sun hits it in the morning. Wicca is the appreciation for the dewdrops on spider webs, the way the gentle breeze caresses your skin on a warm day. It is the blaze of color on the trees when the leaves change due to the turning of the seasons, and the way the snow looks so soft in wintertime. Wicca is the light, the dark and the shadows between. It is nature, the songs that birds sing throughout the day. Wicca understands that you are in the presence of Mother Nature and realizing your role in her family. When you are in Mother Nature's house you are not susceptible to the ego of human technology when it touches your spirit. To be Wiccan means to be a healer, to teach others, to search for the divine, to be a giver and to protect everything. Should you tread this path then you walk it with reverence, light and honesty.

Wicca is a faith and a lifestyle which is founded on the renewal of pre-Christian customs and beliefs which originate in modern day Ireland, Scotland, Wales, England, France and Germany. Unfortunately, the majority of the information surrounding how these ancient cultures lived and worshipped have been obliterated due to the systematic efforts of the medieval Christian church that saw the local traditional beliefs as a threat. However, we are continuing to piece the puzzle pieces together with the information that is accessible.

Due to dedicated archaeological excavations, it looks as though the origins of the Wiccan religion can be dated back to the Palaeolithic cultures who revered a Hunter God and a Fertility Goddess. Cave paintings dating to around 30,000 years ago show stunning illustrations of a human male with a stag's head as well as a pregnant woman upright in a circle which included 11 additional figures. From these illustrations, witchcraft (Wicca, Paganism etc.) has often been claimed to be the oldest unorganized religion in the world ('unorganized religion' being referred to as one without an official canon such as a Torah, Bible, Koran etc.; an 'organized religion' is one that does have an official canon). These prototypes are undoubtedly recognized as Wiccan since the way the Goddess and God have been regarded as the creative force, predating Christianity by around 28,000 years ago.

In earliest times, the practice of Wicca was referred to as "The Craft of the Wise". This was due to those who walked the path was said to have walked in unison with nature, had a profound understanding of herbs and medicines, offered advice in various genres, were considered to be respected and appreciated members of society as a kind of shamanic healer and even leaders. Those who walked this path were all too aware that humanity wasn't superior to that of nature and the creatures that inhabit it, but, instead, understood that humanity is one part of nature, one cog in the unseen and seen aspects which then unite to complete it. It was these people who knew that we must treat the world and everything in it in a kindly manner, giving and taking in equal balance. However, in modern times, there has been a gigantic shift in this balance – where man has taken far more than what he gives back. As such, the world is showing its displeasure through ecological disasters and perhaps our ultimate extinction simply due to a love of power and material wealth.

For the last millennia, the viewpoint of the Witch (or anyone walking this path or lifestyle) has been inaccurately portrayed as an evil heathen and living a corrupt, unrighteous lifestyle. These misconceptions have been believed to originate in a few places which we shall now look at.

During the 5th to 18th centuries, the Christian church developed these stories, these negative stereotypes of those who followed the ancient, nature based religions in order to convert them to Christianity. By transforming a simple Wiccan believer into a terribly wicked character and changing the ancient gods into heathen devils and demons, Christian missionaries were able to scare people into converting. In addition to this, scientific medical began to be a very prosperous position in society. The men who practiced medicine had little to no real knowledge of how a woman's body worked, or anything to do about her monthly cycles. As such, the Witch Hunters who worked for the Church were given credence to their assertions. The new male physicians stood to gain prestige and wealth because the female healers lost their income to them.

Unluckily, these misconceptions, suspicions and falsehoods have been carried on and have largely stayed until today. As such, many of those who follow the path of Wicca have used the name Wicca instead of the term/name Witchcraft due to its history; it is not nice to be persecuted and harassed for a belief or lifestyle which has been largely ascribed in recent years through negative publicity through entertainment and Hollywood just so that they could turn a profit.

Chapter One - What Witchcraft Is

Witchcraft is essentially a faith system which nurtures free thought and individual will, stimulating learning and appreciating and educating oneself on the earth and the natural world, and by doing so, sustaining the divine in everything that lives. By walking this path you are taking responsibility for every action you take and the consequences of those actions. You do not put the blame onto someone else or the divine for any of your weaknesses or mistakes. If you make a mistake and someone gets hurt because of that mistake, then you do not blame anyone but yourself and you must deal with the consequences. There is no whining, no excuses, and no buts. It is about learning and acceptance.

Wiccans accept the cycles of nature, the lunar phases and the ever turning seasons to revere the divine and celebrate our spirituality. Wicca is a faith that one can work in harmony with nature instead of being submissive to other gods, with the intention to live peacefully and with balance in this world.

Wiccans use a range of spells which are centered on love, clarity, healing, wisdom, beauty etc. Potions which are produced are meant to aid in curing a headache, make us feel and look more beautiful etc. Wiccans are ever more looking for new ways to use natural ways to help cure us of ailments given to us by the God and Goddess (also referred to as the Father and Mother), instead of relying on synthetic and mass-produced medicines unless they are an emergency.

Wiccans believe that the spirit of the God and Goddess (or Mother and Father) can be found in everything – in the sun, the sky, the earth, the sea, in animals and also in human beings. As such, we believe that everyone and everything is part of the divine. Wiccans try to honor and respect this belief in all its various embodiments, whether they can be seen or not, felt or not.

Nature is a beautiful thing and Wiccans strive and worship this beautiful aspect of the world through celebrating the natural cycles of the sun, the moon, the stars and the seasons. We look inside ourselves for these cycles which match with the natural world and attempt to live harmoniously with the way the universe lives. We learn from the rivers, streams, lakes, mountains, trees, the ocean, the desert, the various animals and even from our ancestors. Because of this, Wiccans gain a deep veneration and admiration for the world and everything in it.

In addition to this, Wiccans venerate the spirits of the four elements – Earth, Water, Fire and Air – which, when merged together in unison, manifest everything ever created. Taking inspiration from these four elements, we gain a deep understanding of the beat of nature and how they are the very beats to our own individual lives.

Due to the long history of persecution, Wiccans believe that everyone should have the right to practice any religion freely. Wiccans do not believe that our path is the only way to gain spirituality; instead, we believe it is one path out of many which leads us all the same place. We do not have missionaries out seeking to convert new recruits to bring over to the way we think. We listen to people who want to learn about our beliefs, our lifestyles and share what we have learnt so far on this path. Wiccans believe that if you are meant to walk this path then you will find it on your own in your own way and time. Wiccans practice open-mindedness and acknowledgement to every religion in the world providing that these faiths do not persecute other people.

What Witchcraft is Not

Wicca is not a cult. Wiccans do not assert ourselves as a speaker or prophet for the divine, nor do we try to amass a group of other believers to become their leaders.

Wiccans do not worship Satan/the Devil. The Devil was an invention of early Christianity to scared people into joining their faith. As such, Satan has no role in Wicca. Wiccans do not need to produce a terrifying evil personification into forcing us to be good and right and helpful. Wiccans are free to be good and love others because we understand freely that it's the right thing to do.

Wiccans do not perform animal or human sacrifices. The principal tenant is "Harm None"; killing a living creature would be going against everything that we believe in. Wiccans will perform sacrifices, however, but these are such things as sacrificing some free time in order to help others.

Wiccans do not steal or control the life energy of any living creature to attain paranormal or magical powers. Any energy used is taken from deep within ourselves, through our personal relationship with the natural world and the divine.

Wiccans do not utilize the powers of the natural world in order to hex or put a spell or curse on someone. This, just as sacrifices would, be a violation of the basic principles of Wiccan beliefs.

Wiccans believe in the Law of Three. This is basically means that whatever we say or do in this world will come back to us threefold, whether it is good or bad. As a result, a genuine Wiccan follower would not use magic to hurt or control another human being because that action would come back to us three times harder than what we originally did. Not good. Best to play nice after all.

This doesn't mean to imply that Wiccans and Witches are perfect beings – after all, we are human beings just as everyone else is. We make mistakes just like you. Some people can be cruel and vicious, can constantly steal and berate people, and then you have other people who dedicate their time to helping others less fortunate. These kinds of positive, helpful personalities are found in Wiccans along with negative, unhelpful personalities. You see a variety of different positive and negative characters in every religion, including Wiccan.

The majority of Wiccans will continue to strive to educate oneself spiritually, to go forward with purpose and understand that there will consequences to every single action. This is applied before we cast any spells or rituals that could potentially hurt ourselves or anyone else. When we walk the path of the divine and follow the tenant of "Harm None" that everything we do can be beneficial and work in unison with the entire universe.

It can be quite difficult to sum up the beauty and harmony of Wicca in just a couple of paragraphs and even more so when we understand that everyone will experience it in various ways. To understand more about Wicca, continue reading on and you will discover more about our beliefs, our lifestyles and how they can help you. Listen to the words on these pages with a true heart, because when you see how the world works with an open heart and soul it is then that you genuinely begin to see what Wicca is truly all about.

Chapter Two - Various Wiccan Traditions

In this section we will take a look at the various Wiccan traditions that have been identified in recent times.

Gardnerian Wicca

A retired British civil servant known as Gerald B Gardner is considered to be the 'Grandfather' of nearly all the various Wiccan traditions which have arisen in the last 100 years or so. It is said that he was inducted into a coven of witches in 1939 down in the New Forest in southern England. The High Priestess of this coven was known as 'Old Dorothy' Clutterbuck. Ten years later, he produced a book called High Magic's Aid) which was focused on the topic of medieval witchcraft and the craft that the coven was using themselves. Two years later, the Witchcraft laws were repelled and Gerald B. Gardner then issued his Witchcraft Today which sets out a variety of spells, rites and customs of the coven he was initiated into. However, it should be stressed that everything just written has been disagreed with – no one can agree on precisely about these events.

The Gardenrian Wiccan tradition is both a tradition and a family, with a High Priestess leads the coven allowing love, trust and honesty to preside over it. Whilst Wiccans do not have an official Bible or Koran or Torah, we have our own book which has been handed down throughout the generations and it is followed more rigorously than other traditions, but Gardenrian Wiccans have the freedom to adapt and adopt other rites as long as they preserve the original.

Wiccans typically practice naked, practicing binding and scourging, are hierarchal and quite secretive; as such, they are the most controversial out of all the traditions, especially when they are considered to be the first Wiccan tradition in the United States of America.

All the Gardnerian covens are independent of one another and are led by a High Priestess who, when needing guidance, is able to turn to the High Priestess that initiated her; she is known as a queen. As a result, each coven can keep a family tree or lineage and produces a line of proficient and experienced leaders and guides.

Reincarnation and the Wiccan code of conduct ("An it harm none, do as you will") are the two most important rules in this tradition. Gardnerian covens typically pair a male and female together to work with to create balance. The majority of the energy produced in these covens are done so by manifesting the Lord and Lady (the God and Goddess) via the couples dancing, chanting and other such activities.

There are three levels within the Gardnerian tradition (which is typical of most Wiccan traditions); in America, Gardnerians have to be one that is a 3rd degree in order to become a High Priest or High Priestess. These High Priests and Priestesses are in charge of training new members, perform services (also known as circles) and to uphold and continue the Gardnerian tradition.

Much of the controversy which centers on the Gardnerian Wiccan traditions focuses on the origins of the many rites used and the printed material on it. Gardner did portray much of his material as if they had been taken directly from the coven he was initiated into in the New Forest. However, he undoubtedly adapted the information and the rites he may have seen in the coven so much of the information presented has been modified. Later on, the Book of Shadows was published by several individuals including Blake, Yeats and Crowley. Doreen Valiente, who was an initiated member of the Gardnerian Wiccan tradition, produced many books on the subject herself.

There is no question that a lot of information

surrounding Gardnerian Wiccan has been published but they still remain an enigma in the Wiccan world.

Alexandrian Wicca

The Alexandrian Tradition has many similarities with that of Gardnerian, just with the few simple modifications. One of the most recognizable changes is that the Alexandrian Wiccans will use a wand to symbolize the element of air and an athame as the representation of the fire element. Rites are quite formal in this tradition and feature ceremonial magic. A central custom or feature to that of Alexandrian Wicca is that it emphasizes the male and female polarity, especially that of sexuality. The ritual year is typically divided between the Holly Lord and the Oak Lord and the rites feature the dying and resurrected God theme. Just as with the

Gardnerians, the Alexandrians have a High Priestess but it should be noted that the main spokesmen for the Gardnarians and the Alexandrians have been male!

The Alexandrian Tradition was founded by Alex Sanders and his wife, Maxine Sanders, at that time. He asserted that his grandmother had initiated him in the early 1930s. The main supporters of this tradition were Janet and Stewart Fararr and their books go into great detail about the tradition. Despite what you may initially think, the term 'Alexandrian' is not taken from Alex Sanders name, but instead is a reference to ancient Alexandria.

There are many similarities between Gardnarian and Alexandrian Wicca but the latter are far more liberal than the former. Whereas the Gardnarian tradition requires complete nudity during rituals, it is an option for Alexandrians.

Mary Nesnick, an American woman who was brought into both traditions established a new coven which was named Algard. This tradition merges the principles from both traditions into a single coven.

Dianic Wicca

There are two main divisions of Dianic Wicca. The first was established by Morgan McFarland and Mark Roberts in the state of Texas in the United States of America. The goddess is the primary deity in this tradition but it does pay homage to the Horned God as her Divine Consort. Both men and women are welcome here and there are numerous covens found in Texas. They are also known as Old Dianic at times and there are other offshoots of the coven found throughout America but they are not derived from the original.

The second division is occasionally referred to as the Feminist Dianic Witchcraft. It concentrates on the Goddess herself and only female members are permitted. This division is not rigorously organized and performs simple rituals. Members are typically politically feminists and there is a strong lesbian attendance although covens welcome everyone regardless of sexual orientations.

Celtic Wicca (Church of Wicca)

The Church of Wicca (also known as Celtic Wicca) was established by Gavin and Yvonne Frost and they provide long-distance educational programs in their traditions. In recent times, the Frosts have introduced a goddess into their deity arrangement. This branch is sometimes referred to as Baptist Wicca.

This type of Wicca appears to be a combination of high magic and eccentric Wiccan practices with various Celtic elements incorporated into it. As an example, the Church of Wicca uses three circles which fit inside one another – one of salt, one of Sulphur and the other made from herbs –

with runes and symbols drawn in between them. Whereas most Wiccan covens from other traditions will use a black handled athame, this tradition will only use a white handled one. The founders have publicized their tradition far more than others, which has led them to be disapproved by other traditions.

Georgian Wicca

Eccentric is the only way to describe Georgian Wicca. Much of the material given to new members can technically be referred to as Alexandrian, there has never been necessary to walk their road without thinking. The founder of Georgian Wicca was a man known as George Pattison and he was famous for saying, "If it works then use it, if it doesn't, then don't". Their newsletter has featured advice and knowledge from practitioners of all traditions.

Discordianism (Erisian)

The Discordian Tradition, also known as the Erisian Movement) was established when a series of articles and thoughts were brought together by Greg Hill, called *Principia Discordia, or How I Found the Goddess and What I Did to Her When I Found Her'*. This work focuses on how chaos is just as essential as order.

One reoccurring theme in Discordian Wicca is humor; however, although humor can be viewed throughout its teachings, you do find that significant experiences are featured. It illustrates that the everyday humdrum things and the insightful events are both equally important as the other. As a result, it can be incredibly emancipating.

Characterizations of Wicca, Pagan and Witchcraft

Wicca – A contemporary Pagan religion which originates from the initial demonstrations of veneration for nature. Several key themes are the worship of the God and Goddess, belief in reincarnation and the use of magic, ceremonial adherence of natural phenomena and the utilization of magical circles within ceremonial rites.

Wicce – The same as Wicca, but has occasionally referred to as a male practitioner whereas Wicca is applied to women.

Witch – A reference to someone who practices folk magic, with deep knowledge of herbs. Some Wiccans will call themselves a Witch. The term witch has no connection to Satan, Christianity or any other religion.

Witchcraft – The customs and workings of a witch. As with the term 'witch', it has no connection with Satanism or Christianity.

Pagan/ Paganism/Neo-Pagan – This term is the generalization for those who practice Wicca and other nature based or shamanistic or animalistic religions. It can also refer to pre-Christian faith systems in the ancient world.

Chapter Three - The Concept of Deity

As we have already touched upon earlier, Wiccans, Pagans and Witches view the Divine Being, or the Deity, through the manifestation of the God and Goddess. Since our capability to understand the universe and the natural world is restricted somewhat, seeing the Divine through male and female elements aids us in understanding this universal clearer. It does not always mean that we view the Divine as separate beings.

Wiccans acknowledge that various elements of the divine merge together to create the One. As such, we acknowledge and adjust ourselves with the natural world and the energies in it in a way that we are comfortable with, whether that be with others or by ourselves. The next section is an attempt to illuminate this that the majority does concur with.

The Higher Creative Force

The Whole, or the One, is the all-inclusive unity of everything that exists. This includes everything that exists to our restricted knowledge and everything that isn't embodied. The One is simply immeasurable to a point that we cannot understand its immensity.

Oppositions of the One

The God and the Goddess (also known as the Lord and Lady or the Father and Mother) are believed to be the personification of the male and female aspects of the forces of the natural world. Each one is believed to have certain special features that, when merged together, cause the well-balanced formation of life.

This is seen in everything that we see and feel; only when the male and female come together can something exist. As such, this original energy is ubiquitous.

By giving a name to the divine or the male and female aspects of the divine is considered to be unnecessary and certainly not justified by the amount of conflicts and blood spilled because of this naming. Names are simply titles or references that we as people, cultures or particular religions have used for association reasons. It simply doesn't matter whether you call the divine God, Allah or Goddess – the notion is all the same.

Chapter Four - How to Become a Wiccan or Witch

Becoming a Wiccan or a Witch is not something you are typically born into – more likely, you discovering it by chance unless you were born into a family of Wiccans. Quite a number of Wiccans learn that the many beliefs of Wicca see the natural world around them just the same as they did before they learn of Wicca.

Silver RavenWolf describes thus moment of clarification wonderfully in her book entitled *To Ride a Silver Broomstick*. Each of us who finds the path and experiences this 'charge' will do so in our own way; when we feel the energy of the universe flow through us for the initial time then we realize that there is something out there, something that is simply too big for us to understand completely.

Upon reading this, if you find that you are finding certain similarities in what you believe, then there are ways to enhance your understanding and find others that feel the same as you do. I would personally do the following.

Firstly, start reading everything that is available to you. Start learning about the basics of various Wiccan traditions and witchcraft; because when you do you can learn for yourself whether this path is the right one for you.

As you are reading everything that you possibly can – both old texts and modern books – you should with any luck find a connection deep inside. It might be a good idea to write down your journey in some sort of diary. Jot down why you believe Wicca is the path you're meant to tread. What do you hope to gain from Wicca? Is there anything you're scared of as you start your journey? What does the path to the Divine mean to you as an individual, as a society? What is your perception of the God and Goddess?

This is a way of being genuinely truthful with yourself since you will likely not share it with anyone else. Ultimately, this diary, this journal, will become your own Book of Shadows.

Nothing is right or wrong when it comes to your journal, nor is it a test. This is simply a way of helping you understand the path you are taking.

As you start this path, you will learn how to listen to your inner self. The majority of the time your inner self will give you good advice; if you find something that doesn't feel right for you then it probably isn't. If after reading everything that it does feel right, then this is the perfect timing for a dedication rite.

A dedication rite or ceremony is a private and individual affair. It should be arranged to the way you want it to be and includes the things and words that are significant to you. The dedication rite is a ceremony where you dedicate yourself to the path of Wicca and to live harmoniously with nature. It is an oath dedicating your promise to both you and the Divine.

Before you even start thinking of performing spells and working with magic you need to follow the initial two steps. Magic is something extremely powerful and it is essential that you learn everything about it before you start casting spells. Learn about the basic make-up of rites and ceremonies, how to construct a circle, how to call upon the God and Goddess, how to bring forth the energy, what centering and grounding are and lastly, how to close a circle.

Magic is essentially bringing forth and directing the energy found deep within you, the natural world and the Divine. You then merge this energy with concentration to use it. A lot of dedication, commitment, energy and focus go into achieving what you want. But no matter what, you should always keep the first rule of Wicca in your mind and heart:

And It Harm None.

Hollywood has created an image of magic so that the general public thinks its make-believe. Magic is not twisting the natural world in order to attain your desires and shallow wants. If you think magic can conjure you up a new face, or a big fat bank account then Wicca is probably not for you.

Wiccans and witches have suffered long centuries of persecution and bad publicity and it is only in the last few decades that this image is starting to shift. Wiccans do not conjure up hexes and curses on those we feel have wronged us or use magic to instantly give us what we want instead of working for it. Magic is not something out of a Hollywood movie.

As you read and learn about Wicca you will come to understand this. A good way of helping you as you make your first few steps along this path is to undergo some visualization techniques and meditation. You will find if you have a strong ability to focus then it will enhance the strength of your magic. Breathing exercises are a great way of doing this.

If being in a coven sounds more appealing to you, then the majority suggest that you study for a year plus a day before you can be initiated into it. This is so you can learn more about the religion and whether it is a path that you want to take, in addition to allowing the existing members the opportunity in getting to know you. Covens are typically very careful about who they initiate as there are those who walk the road for the wrong purpose. Make sure it is the right one for you.

Chapter Five - Spells

Spells are essentially acts of positive thinking, similar to that of prayers and incantations. Much of the general population doesn't realize that casting spells happens constantly around them. Even without being aware of it, we cast spells every single day. When you focus on something with great passion and desire, you visualize it constantly in your head, in your heart, and when ponder on it, you are, in fact, doing a form of spell casting.

When you cast a spell you are doing more than simply conducting a process which will end up in a particular result – it is also a way of you enhancing your personal growth as you cast each and every single spell.

One of the greatest unexpressed conjectures when you perform a spell is that there is something getting in your way of achieving your desire. If not, then you simply wouldn't require casting a spell. So what is your obstacle?

When you are performing a spell it is important to reflect on why you are doing so. You need to first be aware of the differences between the spell (which is essentially the future) and the present (the moment you are casting or preparing to cast the spell).

For some people, if they can't hear, touch, see or feel anything physical then they don't consider it to be real. Anything that is conjured up in your mind is considered not to be real. But when you believe this, then you are restricting your growth. Your thoughts are in your head – they are real, right? Your dreams are in your head – they are real too. Your feelings can't be physically touched but they, too, are real. The only difference these three examples have is that they have no physical manifestation but it doesn't stop them from being real.

When you cast a spell you are setting things into motion – even just by thinking about casting a spell are you setting the cogs of the universe into motion. When you begin to prepare to cast a spell think about the following questions:

Do I really want this?

What are the possible consequences from this if I cast this spell?

If I do tis spell, what effects in both the short term and long term can I expect?

Once you have answered these questions then you can start preparing your spells.

What kind of spells can we perform?

There is a great deal of spells that we can cast. The majority of the spells you will encounter will be of great help to you on a day to day basis, especially those linked with good health, mental well-being, spiritual enlightenment, trying to figure out who you are and your place in the world, to aid in a good night's sleep etc.

When you perform your spells, it is essential to concentrate on what you want, as you only get what you concentrate on. If you want physical beauty, then focus on physical beauty; if you want purity then concentrate on purity. When you perform a spell you have to be aware that you are accepting the responsibility of any result which may derive from it.

Banishing Spells

Let's take a look at some banishing spells.

Protection against harmful spirits

If you believe you have found yourself with a spirit or paranormal entity that is trying to harm you then you must protect yourself. Here is a spell that will help you get rid of that unwelcome creature.

The first step is to find one or several of the following gemstones – black tourmaline, agate, bloodstone, emerald, black onyx or peridot. These gemstones have a strong reputation in safeguarding individuals from spirits that seek to harm the living. Black tourmaline is the best stone to work with but the others will work as well.

The second stage is to visualize a screen of defensive light enveloping you. This protective light is found deep inside you and can be brought forth through meditative exercises.

On a daily basis, sit down in a quiet location for five minutes and visualize this barrier of protective light encasing you within it; it can be of any color you wish. Say the following words "*I surround myself with a protective barrier. I am safe within it*". Next, feel the warm and the glow from inside you, the light growing brighter as you take your next breath. No wicked spirits or entities can break it.

The next step is to purify the location where you feel the unwanted spirit is most strong, but if it follows you then you can use your own body as the location. If at all possible, try burning some Palo Santo, a type of sacred wood which has been used by shamans to help ward off unwanted spirits. If you can't, then try sage, sandalwood or frankincense. Scatter some sea salt in the location and repeat the subsequent incantation as you purify the area.

"I ask that any unwanted spirits or entities to leave immediately.

Any wicked or negative energies in this area, I ask you to leave.

This is not your home. I send you back to whence you came.

Leave this place now.

Only the healing light and positive energies are allowed here"

Repeat until you are content.

If you find that the first two steps haven't worked properly then you will have to speak with the spirit itself. This can be a dangerous task so ensure you follow the next instructions properly.

First, cast a protective circle and scatter additional sea salt around it for enhanced protection. Your gemstones should either be worn or held in your hands.

Visualize your protective barrier of light to shield you. Then you can communicate with the spirit. You can use the following or create your own.

"To the spirit who currently occupies this space; I am well protected and you cannot hurt me. I am speaking to you with much respect. I do not know why you are here but your presence is negatively affecting my life. There is nothing

here for you. I request that you go. Go back to whence you came. Be at peace".

At the time that you feel safe and secure, then you can close your circle.

Ensure that your gemstones are near to you as regularly as you can. If you feel a negative or unwanted presence, then visualize your protective light barrier encasing you within it and ask the God and Goddess to protect you. If it continues, then seek out a physic or a coven for help.

Wiccan Cleansing Ritual

Our energy levels and our auras are being constantly affected by people, our thoughts and happenings on a day to day basis. No matter how hard we try to remain positive, there will always be times when negative energy will get attached to us and this will then restrict the flow of positive energy. When this happens, we get tired, cranky, irritable and a right pain to deal with. It is important to eat a well-balanced diet, exercise, spend time in our natural surroundings (as opposed to man-made buildings etc.) and perform meditative exercises to help in restoring this delicate flow of positive energy back into our lives. However, there will also be times when we need a little bit of help.

The following cleaning ritual can be conducted any time of the day when you start to feel tired, miserable and depressed.

Firstly, you will need to gather certain items to represent the four elements; sage incense for air; a silver or grey candle for fire; sea salt for earth; and a chalice containing water to represent the water element.

Next, cast your protective circle and light the candle and incense. As the scents perfume the air, perform your meditative exercises and visualize your body relaxing each time you take a breath. The more you relax, the easier it is for your energy to flow and to rid yourself of any negative energy.

The next step is to place your hands above the incense and say *"with air I cleanse myself"*. Visualize the smoke carry the negative energies from your body through your fingertips.

Next, place your hands above the candle (without burning them obviously) and say *"with fire I cleanse myself"*. Visualize the flame burning the negative energies from you.

Next, scoop up the sea salt and allow it to gently fall from your fingers and rub it over your hands and say *"with earth I cleanse myself"*. Feel the negative energy crumble away from your skin.

Finally, submerge your hands in the chalice of water and say *"with water I cleanse myself"*. Feel the water wash the negative energies from you.

If you want to continue to purge any remaining negative energies then you can request that they depart. The best way is to get into a comfortable position and relax your entire body and say the following (or something along the lines of it):

"Any energy which does not positively affect me I ask you to leave

Thank you for being there but now I am sending you home".

It is important that you are firm when you say the words and repeat it several times, being completely aware of how your body feels. When you say these words you can visualize the negatively energies departing from your body – you may even feel your body physically seem lighter than before. Repeat until you feel you have finished.

The last step is quite important. Once you have cleansed yourself of these unwanted negative energies then you will discover that your aura has empty spaces which need to be filled with light or positive energy. If you don't, then the negative energy will find it simple to attach itself to you and then you will need to perform the ritual all over again.

Find a comfortable position and visualize the very top of your head slowly opening itself up. Visualize the divine light gently pouring itself into your head and filling up all the areas that have been previously blocked with negative energy. As you do this say *"I ask that the healing light fills my body"*; repeat this several times before thanking the guardian spirits and, finally, close your circle.

A Spell to Banish Negative Energy

The following spell will cleanse a location and get rid of any undesired negative energies. This particular ritual is great for purifying a room before you cast your protective circle in addition to removing any unwanted energy from a room once disagreeable guests have left.

All you have to do is repeat the following spell either out loud or within your mind as you sketch a pentagram in the air; visualize the pentagram being drawn from pure white light. When the spell has finished, allow the white light to disperse and purify every nook and cranny of the room needing to be cleansed.

"I call you by the names above all other names

I call you by the Lady and the Lord

I call upon the powers of the natural world

I invoke the magic with power and pure heart

Whether held by chains

Or banished to the dark

Never again disturb the children of the gods".

A Spell to Banish an Evil Spirit

Use the next spell to help ward off evil spirits. Whilst the majority of evil spirits can be banished with this spell, it can still be used as a means to hurt them and keep them away until a stronger spell can be used.

Should any spirits attempt to hurt me here

Fight water with water

Fight earth with earth

Fight fire with fire

Fight air with Air

I banish ye into emptiness

I banish ye powers completely

Let all evil spirits flee

And leave me be.

A Spell for Removing Anger

This quick and easy spell is a great way of helping you get rid of unwanted anger without having to perform a full ritual. It can be performed for yourself or for someone else.

You can add a special element to this spell – all you have to do is to take a stone (any stone will do) and hold it in your hand. As you say the words, visualize all that anger pouring into the stone. Once the anger has completely left your body and is now trapped into that stone, all you need to do is cast it away. The best place is to throw it into water, such as a lake, river or even a stream – and that way the water will naturally cleanse it.

Repeat the following words as you visualize the anger leaving you.

To the Guardian Spirits who dwell in the West

Who oversees the oceans and the seas

Allow this anger to dissolve

Cast it out forever,

So mote it be.

Beauty Spells

Let's face it; we all want to feel and look beautiful (some days more than others). Let's take a look at some beauty spells that we can cast.

Ritual for Self-Love

Life is better and far more fun when we love ourselves and our roles in this world. Unfortunately, it can take years to understand that it is a choice whether we love ourselves or not and after that, we have to learn to put that understanding into actual practice.

The very best state of being is love and it begins inside us. We all know the saying that when you love yourself then other people will love us.

When you learn to love yourself your viewpoint is much clearer and you gain a deeper sense of compassion – clarity and compassion are two vital components when it comes to magic and the divine. As such, it is necessary to love yourself. The following is a great self-love meditation exercise which will help you learn to love and respect your entire being.

It is recommended that you practice this meditative exercise on a regular basis. After a while, you will be able to perform it anywhere and anytime of the day – even whilst waiting for the bus!

Find somewhere comfortable and relaxing to start your meditative exercises. Acknowledge any thoughts that come into your mind but don't dwell on them and instead, concentrate on taking in long, deep breaths. If anything should pop into your mind and linger there, dismiss it and concentrate of being aware of your entire body and your breathing.

Instead of visualizing anything outwards of your body, look deep within your chest – this is the location where love emanates from, whether it be self-love, romantic love, physical love or parent love, it all stems from here.

Instead of visualizing your breath leaving your body, see it being inhaled right into your heart. It may feel like a ball of pure light pulsating and expanding every time you inhale. As you breathe in, you absorb the energy around you and every time you breathe out, your heart grows bigger until ultimately it bursts open and fills the room with pure, loving and healing light.

As this light bursts and fills the room, say the following incantation.

"Love can be found everywhere in the universe

Love can be found inside of me

I see myself for the wondrous soul that I am

I see the role I play in this world

Grant me the assistance to know the path I tread

Grant me the clarity to see my true worth

53

Grant me the ability to love myself

As I have the ability to love others

So mote it be".

Inhale and exhale slowly and gently, feeling the strength and conviction behind the words you have just spoken. If you feel any conflict when you say these words, try to understand where this conflict is located in your body. When you next do the ritual, concentrate on sending healing energies from your heart onto this location; remember that when you say this incantation aloud you are giving them far more strength and power.

Weight Loss Spell

There are certain spells which are beneficial for helping boost your metabolism which will help burn those nasty calories quicker. You won't have the desired weight loss instantaneously, but within time you will see a vast improvement. Enhance the power of this spell by ensuring that you are eating a well-balanced and nutritious diet and take the time to exercise on a daily basis.

To perform this spell you will require a red candle, a small pouch (ideally it should be red or orange), and a teaspoon of cayenne pepper, ground cinnamon and ground ginger. If you can't get all three ingredients then just once will suffice. The spell should be cast during a waning moon.

Firstly, center and then ground yourself followed by casting your circle. Light the red candle and position your ingredients before you. Whilst the candle is burning, visualize the heat from the flame heating your body. Gaze into the flame and visualize your body accepting the characteristics of fire. As you see the fire burning the candlewax visualize it burning away all the excess body fat stored away inside of you.

As you are visualizing this, repeat this spell:

"Fire, rise up from deep inside of me

Burn this unnecessary weight

Flame, warm my body

Burn away this unwanted weight.

Pour the spices into your pouch and close it up and circle it above the candle three times and imagine that it is absorbing the warmth of the flame. Then say: *"So mote it be"*. Blow out the candle and then close your circle. It is important to keep the pouch as near to your body for the period that you want to lose weight – the most useful place is located on or near your stomach.

Every time you finish a meal, take the pouch into your left hand and imagine the heat from the contents being absorbed into your fingertips, up your arm and coursing into your stomach. You will notice that your body will start burning the calories much quicker than before which ultimately helps you to lose weight in the long term.

Wiccan Beauty Spell

If you want to be seen as beautiful by others then firstly you need to feel beautiful to yourself. Beauty is found within and then outside. This spell will help you boost your self-confidence, happiness and health, all of which are the essential components of being beautiful.

This spell requires a gemstone to help boost confidence such as Honey Opal, Kunzite or Sodalite, as well as an athame (if you don't possess one then you can use another knife). Since red is the color of fire and physical love, you should wear something red or have something large and red close to hand as you perform the spell.

Stand before your altar or your working table in a strong, self-assured stance. Breathe slowly and deeply, allowing your body to relax. As you exhale, imagine the stress and anxieties leaving your body. If any stray thoughts should come into your mind acknowledge them but ignore them, and then focus on the spell.

Keep your posture strong and then take your athame and direct the blade to the ground. Say, *"May I attract the Earth's poise and vivacity"*.

Clutch the athame to your bosom and visualize the energy of the earth soaking into your body. Then direct the blade to the sky and say, *"May I attract the Wind's strength and liveliness"*. Clutch the athame to your bosom and feel the strength and the playful nature of the winds and breezes course through your body.

Next, position your stone over your Solar Plexus – this is the location where your inner strength and your self-confidence inhabit. As you position it over this area, say the following:

"I energize the heart of my body

Let the flames burn inside of me

I will feel the power of myself

All throughout my body".

Repeat this incantation several times, visualizing the stone filling your body with a yellow or orange tone of light.

Then position the stone over your Third Eye (in the middle of your forehead) and repeat the following:

Moon and Sun, illuminate the skies

Gift me with from up on high

Everlasting beauty until I die

All is done.

So mote it be.

Repeat several times, imagining the stone liquefying and submerging your body in balmy, silky oil. Keep the stone close to you over the next few weeks and you will feel yourself growing more confident in yourself and more beautiful.

Mirror Glamour Spell

This is a type of glamour spell which will aid you in enhancing the way you look depending on how you want to look. The best time to perform this spell is during the waxing moon and should be repeated over the next 13 nights.

This glamour spell requires three pink candles, a mirror and rose essential oil. Firstly, you will need to rub down the candles with the oils (you can use gloves if the oils irritate your skin).

Light all of the candles and place them before you. Ensure that no other lights can be seen other than the candles. Sit in front of the mirror, gazing intently into it. Begin by visualizing a rose tinted light encasing your entire body.

Visualize this light showering yourself in beauty and transforming

"Sacred light

Here tonight

I call on the second sight

Grant me [say what you want here]

Fill with your light

Sacred fire

Hear my desire

By the power of the three

Let all see

Let all see

And it is done

So mote it be".

It is important that you perform this spell every day for 13 nights. If you don't then you will have to wait until the next waxing moon and re-do it all over again.

A Simple Truth Spell

The following spells are usual when you want to find out the truth behind something. If you feel as though someone is keeping something secret from you, or if you want to illuminate a situation, then this is the ideal spell to cast.

This simple truth spell requires a white or purple candle and a purified lapis lazuli gemstone – this can be done before you perform the spell. Submerge the gemstone in water with a sprinkling of sea salt, or else you can purify it by placing the gemstone over a lighted stick of incense. Both the sea salt and the smoke are great ways to purify an object.

Centre and then ground yourself, light the

candle and use the flame before you to meditate. Empty your mind and then take the gemstone into your hand. Visualise a pure white flame enlarging each time you breathe, until the light illuminates everything in the room. At this point, pour the white light into the stone and repeat the spell:

Truth, clarify, illumination

Reveal all unto me

No longer hidden, no longer secret

It is done

So mote it be.

Now close the circle. Keep the stone in a white cloth or pouch and place it under your pillow. When you sleep, the truth that you seek will be revealed in your dreams.

Conclusion

-By reading this book, I hope you have gained an insight into the history, the beliefs and practices of the Wiccan religion. Hopefully you will have learnt that Wicca is not something to be feared or hated; it is a spiritual path that will help you enhance your connection to the divine and the natural world in which we live in.

Wicca is an individual path to the Divine, but can be shared with others in a coven. There are many paths which can lead us to the Divine, Wicca being one of them. This guide will help you begin your journey to the Divine through helpful practices and spells.

Blessed Be.